Teddy Bears' Picnic Cookbook

TEDDY BEARS' PICNIC COOKBOOK

by Abigail Darling

illustrated by Alexandra Day

Green Tiger Press
A Division of Laughing Elephant Books
3645 Interlake Avenue North
Seattle, Washington 98103
1-800-354-0400

www.LAUGHINGELEPHANT.com

ISBN 1-883211-60-3

INTRODUCTION

Picnics are a way for teddy bears and children to enjoy cooking, eating, and spending time out of doors. Because teddy bears have paws, not hands, the recipes in this book are simple and easy to make, but an adult is needed to help with sharp knives and hot stoves. Each picnic will serve four children or teddies.

With some planning, a picnic can be fun at any time of year. Where can you have a picnic? There are all the places you are used to thinking about, like parks and the beach – but how about your backyard or porch, or even indoors? If you use your imagination, you will discover that the world is full of possible picnic locations.

Sometimes teddy bears don't have time to prepare a whole picnic, so they just have a simple meal like bread, cheese, and fruit, or they add something ready-made like cookies or pudding cups. A picnic doesn't have to be fancy to be fun. We have included easy options to many of the recipes for those times when you want something easier.

Tips to Help You Be a Good, Safe Chef

COOKING

- read the recipe all the way through before you begin, to make sure you understand it and that you have everything you need
- wear an apron, and wash your hands before you begin
- take out everything you will be using and measure it
- if any fruits or vegetables are called for, wash them

- ask a grown-up to help when you need to use the oven or stove, any sharp utensils, or any appliances such as blenders
- when using a knife or peeler, go slowly and cut away from your body
- always use potholders when handling hot dishes or pots
- turn off the oven or stove as soon as you are finished with using it
- when cooking on top of the stove, point pot handles toward the center, so that they cannot be easily knocked off

CLEANUP

Be sure to leave the kitchen clean so that grown ups will be glad to let you use the kitchen again. And always be sure not to leave anything behind at your picnic spot. Make it look as if you were never there, and if other people have left trash, pick that up, too.

PACKING

To go on a picnic, you will need something to put the food in. If you don't have a picnic basket, you could use a backpack, a tote bag, or the basket of your bicycle.

The recipes in this book give instructions for packing, but here are some more tips to help you pack food. Keep hot things hot and cold things cold using insulated bags and carriers, cold packs and ice. This is especially important if you are going to eat more than an hour after you pack the food.

- salads, soft fruit, and any other delicate items should be packed in plastic containers with lids–liquids, such as soups or beverages, should be packed in a thermos
- sandwiches or bread can be wrapped in plastic wrap, waxed paper, or aluminum foil, or put in small plastic bags
- fruits, vegetables, cookies, or crackers can be put in plastic bags
- when packing up your picnic food, be sure to put anything that could be crushed, like fruit, cookies or chips, on top
- if using a thermos for hot soup or beverages, it is a good idea to warm the inside of the thermos with hot tap water, leave it for a few minutes, then pour out the water right before you are ready to add your soup or other liquid
- be sure to take along plates or bowls, eating utensils, and cups
- and don't forget to bring napkins

BREAKFAST PICNIC

It may seem that breakfast is not a picnic meal, but a morning picnic can be fun. The world is beautiful early in the day, and you will see different things from those you would see in the afternoon. Parks and other public places will be less crowded. Teddy bears like to go on morning picnics in the summertime, so they can enjoy the sunshine before it is too hot for them in their furry coats. This picnic is quick to prepare.

MENU

RECIPES	ITEMS TO BRING ALONG
Scrambled Egg Sandwiches	Oranges
Smoothies	
EASY ALTERNATIVE:	
Yogurt Drinks or Milk	

SCRAMBLED EGG SANDWICHES

After you have made these sandwiches once, try a little creativity. Add some chopped vegetables, like tomatoes or green onions, to the eggs. Or place a slice of ham on top of the
eggs and cheese. You should make these just before you leave for your picnic, so they'll
still be warm when you eat them.

EQUIPMENT

> bowl, fork, measuring cup, frying pan,
> wooden spoon, lid to cover
> frying pan, toaster, grater (unless
> cheese is pre-grated)

TO PACK

> aluminum foil

INGREDIENTS

> 6 eggs
> 1/4 cup milk
> 2 tablespoons (1/4 stick) butter
> 1 cup grated cheese
> 4 English muffins
> soft butter for buttering muffins

Grate cheese, if necessary. Break the eggs into the bowl, add milk, and mix up with fork.
Over low heat, melt butter in frying pan. Pour the egg/milk mixture into the pan. Stir
the eggs gently with wooden spoon over low heat while they cook. When the eggs are
no longer runny and are cooked to your liking, sprinkle with the grated cheese and put a
lid on the frying pan. Turn off heat.

Now toast and butter muffins. Put equal amounts of the egg/cheese mixture on four of
the English muffin halves, then cover with the other four English muffins halves. Wrap
each sandwich tightly in aluminum foil to keep it warm.

SMOOTHIES

Smoothies are one of those things that taste good and are good for you. This drink will give you energy for the day ahead. You can use any combination of fruit, juice, and yogurt that sounds good to you. Part of learning to cook is learning to imagine what something will taste like before you actually taste it. Here are some suggestions to help you begin:

> orange juice, vanilla yogurt, banana
> cranberry juice cocktail, blueberry yogurt, blueberries
> apple juice, strawberry yogurt, strawberries

EQUIPMENT

> blender, measuring cup, knife for cutting up fruit

TO PACK

> thermos

INGREDIENTS

> 1 cup fruit cut up into medium pieces, can be fresh or frozen
> 1 cup fruit juice
> 1 cup milk
> 1 eight ounce container of yogurt
> 4 ice cubes (you don't need these if you use frozen fruit)

You should ask an adult for assistance using the blender. Place all the ingredients in the blender jar, and put the lid on. Turn on the blender and blend until smooth. Pour into thermos.

RAINY DAY PICNIC

It may seem as though rainy days and picnics don't fit together very well. But teddy bears are optimists, which means they try to find joy in everything. They know that rain is important for plants and flowers, and from flowers comes honey.

A wet afternoon is a fine time to read, play games, or draw pictures. Another good activity (and a favorite of always-hungry teddies!) is to plan, cook, and eat a meal. Spread a blanket on the floor, and enjoy this warming indoor picnic.

MENU

RECIPES
Vegetable Soup
EASY ALTERNATIVE:
Canned Soup
Baked Apples
EASY ALTERNATIVE:
Gingersnaps

ITEMS TO BRING ALONG
Bread or crackers
Milk

VEGETABLE SOUP

EQUIPMENT

large pot with lid, measuring cups and spoons, wooden spoon, ladle, small bowl or cup for testing doneness

INGREDIENTS

3 tablespoons olive oil
2 teaspoons Italian seasoning (a mixture of herbs like oregano, thyme and basil)
2 cups chicken, beef or vegetable stock
2 cups of water
1 small (8 ounce) can garbanzo or kidney beans, drained
1 large can (15 ounce) tomato sauce
2 cups frozen mixed vegetables (a 10-ounce package)
I cup small pasta shells or macaroni, uncooked

Place all the ingredients in the pot. Mix with the wooden spoon, put lid on the pot, and heat over medium low heat for 30 minutes. Stir and check halfway through the cooking time; if it seems like there isn't enough water, add more a half-cup at a time. When cooking time is up, spoon a little of the soup into the small bowl or cup. Let it cool a little, so you don't burn yourself, and taste, making sure the pasta is cooked. If you need to cook it a little more, check again after 5 more minutes. When done, serve the soup in bowls using the ladle.

BAKED APPLES

EQUIPMENT

8-inch cake pan, apple corer, measuring cups and spoons, small bowl,
oven mitts, fork

INGREDIENTS

soft butter for buttering the pan
4 apples, washed and cored (you may need adult help in coring the apples)
1/2 stick (1/4 cup) butter
4 tablespoons brown sugar
I teaspoon cinnamon
1 cup water

Preheat oven to 350 degrees

Butter the pan by rubbing it all over with soft butter (a small piece of wax paper – or a
piece of the butter wrapper – is good for this) then place apples in pan. Cut the 1/2 stick
of the butter into four pieces, and put one piece inside each of the apples. Mix the brown
sugar, cinnamon, and water in bowl, and pour over the apples. Bake for 30 minutes.
Wearing oven mitts, test an apple to see if it is soft all the way through by poking it with
fork. Remove pan from oven when apples are done. Serve warm – ice cream is a delicious addition.

Teddies like all kinds of parties and celebrations, but they truly love tea parties. At a tea party, teddy bears can eat sweets, including their favorite, honey. Lady bears wear their lacy white gloves and hats with flowers; gentlemen bears often put on top hats and everyone speaks to one another of important things and uses their best manners. You can give a tea party for your friends, family, or teddies. Try to make everything as pretty as possible with flowers, tablecloths, and nice teacups and saucers (but remember to ask permission!) This party needs to be on a table; a porch or backyard picnic table is perfect.

MENU

RECIPES	ITEMS TO BRING ALONG
Little Sandwiches	Hot Tea with Milk and Honey
Strawberries and Cream	*EASY ALTERNATIVE:*
	Iced tea, sun tea or instant
	Cookies – your favorite kind

LITTLE SANDWICHES

These are also called tea sandwiches, and eating them is one of the few times that not eating the crusts of the bread is allowed. Most children like peanut butter, and teddy bears love it, but if you feel adventurous you could try something a little more sophisticated. Here are some other tea sandwich suggestions:

> thinly sliced cucumbers on buttered bread
> cream cheese mixed with chopped up green onions on bread
> thinly sliced tomatoes and ham on buttered bread

EQUIPMENT

> bread knife, cutting board, knife for spreading peanut butter

INGREDIENTS

> 10 slices bread – thin is best
> smooth peanut butter
> jam or honey (if desired)

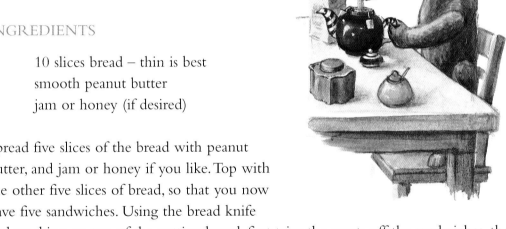

Spread five slices of the bread with peanut butter, and jam or honey if you like. Top with the other five slices of bread, so that you now have five sandwiches. Using the bread knife and working on top of the cutting board, first trim the crusts off the sandwiches, then cut into the patterns pictured below. Serve on a large plate.

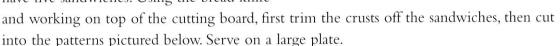

STRAWBERRIES AND CREAM

EQUIPMENT

small knife, cutting board, colander, large jar with lid

INGREDIENTS

1 cup heavy cream
2 tablespoons sugar
1 regular size basket of strawberries (about 2 cups)
sugar for sprinkling on strawberries

Put the cream and 2 tablespoons of sugar in a large jar and put the lid on tightly. Give it a shake, to blend in the sugar, put in the freezer while you work on the strawberries. Be careful not to forget about the cream, you want it to be very cold, but not frozen.

Wash and drain the strawberries in the colander. Working on the cutting board, cut the green top off each berry and cut in half (if they are really big strawberries, you may need to cut them in half again.) Place the berries in small bowls or cups (clear ones look very pretty) and sprinkle with a little sugar. Take the jar out of the freezer and make sure the lid is on TIGHT. Shake the jar up and down until cream is about the consistency of soft ice cream. This will take about 5 minutes, depending on how thick you like your cream. When finished shaking, pour cream on top of strawberries in bowls and serve with cookies.

PICNIC
á la
FRANCE

Teddy bears and the people of France are a lot alike. They like to wear fashionable clothes, especially hats. Eating and preparing good food is something both teddies and French people enjoy a great deal. French food is famous all over the world because it is so delicious.

Teddies, who like to seem worldly, love French food. The little bears study fancy cookbooks, and try out new recipes. You can expand your culinary horizons with this simple French outdoor meal. Remember to take along your "chapeaux" and say "Bon appetit!"

MENU

RECIPES
Croissant or Baguette Sandwiches
Truffles au Chocolat (chocolate candies)
  EASY ALTERNATIVE:
  Small Chocolate Bars

ITEMS TO BRING ALONG
Grape Juice or Eau Minerale (mineral water)

CROISSANT OR BAGUETTE SANDWICHES

Croissants are a delicious type of buttery bread that are loved by the French and anyone else who eats them. Baguettes, which are long skinny loaves of bread, are also very French and very tasty.

EQUIPMENT

bread knife, cutting board, knife for spreading condiments, knife for cutting cheese unless it is pre-sliced

TO PACK

aluminum foil, plastic wrap, or sandwich bags

INGREDIENTS

4 croissants or 1 baguette
4 slices of cheese and/or 4 slices of ham
lettuce and tomato (if desired)
mustard, butter, mayonnaise (if desired)

Using the bread knife and working on the cutting board, slice the croissants in half lengthwise or slice the baguette into 4 pieces, then cut each piece in half lengthwise. Spread the croissant/baguette halves with whatever condiments you would like. Then place a slice of cheese and/or a slice of ham on the four croissant/baguette halves. Add leaves of lettuce and slices of tomato, if you'd like, and top with remaining four croissant or baguette halves. Wrap in foil or plastic wrap or place in plastic bags.

TRUFFLES AU CHOCOLAT

Truffles are named after a rare and delicious kind of mushroom. In France mushroom truffles are hunted by pigs who sniff the ground to find them. These truffles are made with chocolate. Who doesn't like chocolate better than mushrooms?

EQUIPMENT

heatproof bowl, measuring cups and spoons, oven mitts, shallow bowl, fork, spoon, plate

TO PACK

small plastic container with lid

INGREDIENTS

1 cup chocolate chips
1/2 stick (1/4 cup) butter cut into small pieces
1/2 teaspoon vanilla
1/4 cup powdered sugar
2 tablespoons cocoa

Place chocolate chips, vanilla, and butter in heatproof bowl. Microwave on high for 1 minute. Using oven mitts, take the bowl out of the microwave and stir with the fork to see if the chocolate is all melted, if it is not, microwave another 10 seconds and check again, repeating until chocolate is completely melted. When chocolate is melted, mix up chocolate and butter mixture with the fork until smooth and completely combined. Cover bowl with plastic wrap and put in the refrigerator for 1 hour or until cold and firm. Mix cocoa/powdered sugar in the shallow bowl. Using the spoon, spoon out about a tablespoon of chocolate, and roll it between your hands to make a ball. Don't handle them for too long, though, because the heat of your hands will melt the chocolate. Roll each ball in the sugar/cocoa mixture, and put on plate. Chill until they are hard again, about a half hour, then put in their container. Keep refrigerated until you are ready to leave for your picnic, and keep them cool or they will melt.

WARM WINTERY PICNIC

Teddy bears are well-dressed for winter, which they enjoy very much. Often they will be caught frolicking in the snow, and when there are wet footprints on the floor, sometimes teddies are to blame.

Picnics in winter can be great fun. Dress warmly, and bring warm food. Find a dry place to sit, or bring something to sit on. If you see some teddy bears nearby, take them for a sleigh ride or help them build a snowman.

MENU

RECIPES
Cheesy Baked Potatoes
Honey Hot Chocolate
  EASY ALTERNATIVE:
  Instant hot chocolate or chocolate milk

ITEMS TO BRING ALONG
Graham Crackers

CHEESY BAKED POTATOES

EQUIPMENT

Cookie sheet, oven mitts, sharp knife, cutting board, bowl, fork, measuring cup, spoon, grater (unless cheese is pre-grated)

TO PACK

aluminum foil

INGREDIENTS

4 small potatoes
1 cup of grated cheese
4 tablespoons (1/2 stick) cold butter cut into 8 pieces
Preheat oven to 450 degrees

After washing potatoes, poke each one two or three times with the fork. Place on cookie sheet and bake potatoes for 45 minutes, or until fork goes in easily. Wearing the oven mitts to protect your hands, take potatoes out of oven and put on cutting board. Still wearing the mitts - cut each potato in half lengthwise with the sharp knife. Place 1/4 of grated cheese on one half of each potato. Put 2 pieces of butter on top of cheese. Press two potato halves (one with cheese, one without) back together, and wrap each one tightly in aluminum foil to keep them warm. The heat of the potato will melt the cheese while you are on your way to the picnic.

HONEY HOT CHOCOLATE

EQUIPMENT

medium-sized pan, whisk, measuring cups
and spoons

TO PACK

thermos

INGREDIENTS

4 tablespoons cocoa
4 tablespoons honey
4 cups milk

Put cocoa in the pan with a little of the milk (about 3 tablespoons) and mix with whisk until there are no cocoa lumps. Add the remaining milk and the honey. Heat over low heat, stirring occasionally with the whisk, for 5 minutes until cocoa is hot but not boiling. Pour cocoa into thermos. Be sure to take along plastic or metal mugs. Warm cups feel nice on cold hands or paws.

BIRTHDAY PICNIC

Teddy bears, like children, celebrate their birthdays with their families. But that is no reason not to have an extra birthday party for a friend or family member. Toys and pets have birthdays, too, and would enjoy a party. A birthday party needs a cake, which is a big job for a teddy bear. Maybe an adult could help you make a cake, or buy one from a market or bakery? Serve the cake with ice cream, or just have ice cream all by itself. Use pretty paper plates and napkins, and bring along party hats to make your birthday picnic festive.

MENU

RECIPES
Vegetable and Cheese Pitas
Fruit Fizz Punch
  EASY ALTERNATIVE:
  Soda or Juice

ITEMS TO BRING ALONG
Pretzels and Potato Chips
Cake and/or Ice Cream

Pita bread is from the Middle East and Mediterranean, and is eaten a lot in countries such as Greece, Lebanon, and Israel. It forms a natural pocket when it bakes, and makes wonderful sandwiches. You can change this recipe to suit your own taste, using different cheeses or vegetables, adding meat, or maybe using a ranch dressing instead of Italian.

bowl, fork, knife, cutting board, measuring cup and spoons, grater (unless cheese is pre-grated

aluminum foil or plastic wrap (if this picnic is being held near home, the sandwiches can just be put on a plate)

1 1/2 cups grated cheese
1 carrot, grated
1 stalk celery, cut into small pieces
I tomato, cut into small pieces
4 tablespoons Italian salad dressing
4 pita breads

Grate carrot and cheese, if necessary. Cut up the vegetables. Place all the ingredients except the pita bread in a bowl, and mix lightly with fork. Cut the pita breads in half, and in each half spoon in some cheese/vegetable mixture. Wrap each pair of halves in aluminum foil or put on a plate.

no cooking utensils are needed for this recipe

a large, resealable plastic bag for the ice, or bowl if this picnic is close to home

1 liter soda
1 quart fruit juice or fruit drink
ice

Take along on your picnic the soda and juice, and some ice cubes. Put some ice in each picnicker's glass, and then pour in equal amounts of juice and soda. Some good juice and soda mixtures would be:

vanilla soda and peach or apricot juice
ginger ale and cranberry juice cocktail
club soda and fruit punch

MORE PICNIC FOODS

SANDWICHES

Sandwiches, of course, are the most popular and easy picnic food. Here are lists of suggestions for different fillings and breads

FILLINGS

Peanut butter and jam, jelly,
 raisins, or bananas
Cheese
Bologna, or other sandwich meats,
or fake meat products
Meat loaf
Tuna, egg, or chicken salad

BREADS

White, wheat, sourdough, or rye bread
Raisin bread
Pita bread
Bagels
English muffins
Rolls
Croissants
Flour tortillas or "wraps"

MAIN DISHES OTHER THAN SANDWICHES

Soup in a thermos
English muffin pizza
Burritos or tacos
Macaroni and cheese

SIDE DISHES AND SNACKS

Carrot and celery sticks
Green salad
Macaroni or potato salad
Small bags of chips or pretzels
Trail mix (dried fruit and nuts)
Fresh fruit

DESSERTS

Cookies
Small candy bars
Puddings cups